EDITH IN THE DARK

by Philip Meeks

|| SAMUEL FRENCH ||

Copyright © 2015 by Philip Meeks
All Rights Reserved

EDITH IN THE DARK is fully protected under the copyright laws of the British Commonwealth, including Canada, the United States of America, and all other countries of the Copyright Union. All rights, including professional and amateur stage productions, recitation, lecturing, public reading, motion picture, radio broadcasting, television, online/digital production, and the rights of translation into foreign languages are strictly reserved.

ISBN 978-0-573-11114-3

concordtheatricals.co.uk
concordtheatricals.com

FOR PRODUCTION ENQUIRIES
United Kingdom and World
excluding North America
licensing@concordtheatricals.co.uk
020-7054-7298

North America
info@concordtheatricals.com
1-866-979-0447

Each title is subject to availability from Concord Theatricals,
depending upon country of performance.

CAUTION: Professional and amateur producers are hereby warned that *EDITH IN THE DARK* is subject to a licensing fee. The purchase, renting, lending or use of this book does not constitute a licence to perform this title(s), which licence must be obtained from the appropriate agent prior to any performance. Performance of this title(s) without a licence is a violation of copyright law and may subject the producer and/or presenter of such performances to penalties. Both amateurs and professionals considering a production are strongly advised to apply to the appropriate agent before starting rehearsals, advertising, or booking a theatre. A licensing fee must be paid whether the title is presented for charity or gain and whether or not admission is charged.

This work is published by Samuel French, an imprint of Concord Theatricals Ltd.

The Professional Rights in this play are controlled by Concord Theatricals, Aldwych House, 71-91 Aldwych, London, WC2B 4HN.

No one shall make any changes in this title for the purpose of production. No part of this book may be reproduced, stored in a retrieval system, scanned, uploaded, or transmitted in any form, by any means, now known or yet to be invented, including mechanical, electronic, digital, photocopying, recording, videotaping, or otherwise, without the prior written permission of the publisher. No one shall share this title, or part of this title, to any social media or file hosting websites.

The moral right of Philip Meeks to be identified as author of this work has been asserted in accordance with Section 77 of the Copyright, Designs and Patents Act 1988.

USE OF COPYRIGHTED MUSIC

A licence issued by Concord Theatricals to perform this play does not include permission to use the incidental music specified in this publication. In the United Kingdom: Where the place of performance is already licensed by the PERFORMING RIGHT SOCIETY (PRS) a return of the music used must be made to them. If the place of performance is not so licensed then application should be made to PRS for Music (www.prsformusic.com). A separate and additional licence from PHONOGRAPHIC PERFORMANCE LTD (www.ppluk.com) may be needed whenever commercial recordings are used. Outside the United Kingdom: Please contact the appropriate music licensing authority in your territory for the rights to any incidental music.

USE OF COPYRIGHTED THIRD-PARTY MATERIALS

Licensees are solely responsible for obtaining formal written permission from copyright owners to use copyrighted third-party materials (e.g., artworks, logos) in the performance of this play and are strongly cautioned to do so. If no such permission is obtained by the licensee, then the licensee must use only original materials that the licensee owns and controls. Licensees are solely responsible and liable for clearances of all third-party copyrighted materials, and shall indemnify the copyright owners of the play(s) and their licensing agent, Concord Theatricals Ltd., against any costs, expenses, losses and liabilities arising from the use of such copyrighted third-party materials by licensees.

IMPORTANT BILLING AND CREDIT REQUIREMENTS

If you have obtained performance rights to this title, please refer to your licensing agreement for important billing and credit requirements.

For Dale Meeks (1974-2023)

HARROGATE THEATRE

Edith in the Dark was originally commissioned by Harrogate Theatre and its first production took place in Harrogate Studio Theatre in December 2013 with the following cast and creative team:

Edith Nesbit **Blue Merrick**
Mr. Guasto **Scott Ellis**
Biddy Thricefold **Janet Amsden**
Director **Keith Hukin**
Designer **Alex Swarbrick**
Sound Designer **Gerrard Fletcher**

It was then revived in March 2015 at Harrogate Theatre in association with Reform Theatre with the following cast and creative team:

Edith Nesbit **Blue Merrick**
Mr. Guasto **Patrick Neyman**
Biddy Thricefold **Nicky Goldie**
Director **Keith Hukin**
Designer **Alex Swarbrick**
Lighting Designer **Arnim Friess**
Sound Designer **Gerrard Fletcher**

An abridged version of the play was presented at the Edinburgh Fringe Festival in August 2015 (Momentum Venues) with the following cast and creative team:

Edith Nesbit **Blue Merrick**
Mr. Guasto **Scott Ellis**
Biddy Thricefold **Rebecca Mahon**
Director **Keith Hukin**
Designer **Alex Swarbrick**
Sound Designer **Gerrard Fletcher**

NOTES ON THE STAGING

The setting and costume should be kept as simple as possible. The transformations in the play from role to role should be done through performance alone. No change of costume is required and props unless stated in the text should be kept to a minimum. The strength of the production is in the hands of the actors, supplemented by strong support from sound and lighting.

SETTING

Christmas eve 1909.

We're in one of the cluttered attic rooms of the large town house Edith Nesbit shares with her husband and strange family.

The staging should be simple. Props found in the attic can be employed but the character transformations should be done without costume changes. The horrors employed in the stories should be reacted to rather than seen, music and lighting being used to crank up the tension.

When we meet E Nesbit her most accomplished tales for children have been published and celebrated, though many still believe her to be a man. She has endured years of marriage to the philandering Hubert Bland, but hasn't been without extra marital dalliances of her own. She's also very recently buried her young son.

CHARACTERS

EDITH NESBIT – In her forties, Edith is astute and brilliant but unhappy. She's quick witted and has an eye for a younger man. She's a very modern woman for the era in which she lives. But almost everything she does is a diversion from her own personal heartbreak and secrets.

MR. GUASTO – Tall, strident and handsome in his late twenties. He arrives uninvited but when he helps Edith with an ailing guest gets more than he bargained for. He's a huge fan of Edith's work, but since he has a terrible fear of the grave, is not expecting the night that lies ahead of him.

BIDDY THRICEFOLD – Mid fifties or above. Biddy is a terrible housekeeper and rather too fond of her own home-made spiced punch. She loves Edith and despite the banter the feeling is mutual. She's more of a companion than a servant, and although the part has been written for an older actor could be played by someone the same age as Edith. The character supplies a lot of the humour in the early part of the play but has a terrible secret of her own that she finally finds a way to share.

All three actors also play the roles featured in the stories within the play regardless of gender or age.

ACT ONE

Scene One

Christmas Eve 1909.

Music – God Rest Ye Merry Gentlemen *if the play is being presented near Christmas. If not and the festive aspect of the story is to be played down, something equally as eerie...*

We find **EDITH** *and* **GUASTO** *in* **EDITH**'s *attic writing room. A festive gathering is taking place below in the main body of the house. We hear bursts of music and muffled laughter.*

MR GUASTO *is looking at a vase filled with dead lilies. There are several on display in the room.* **EDITH** *notices him...*

EDITH I don't like to throw them away. I won't. It's important to keep them close. For me at least. It drives everyone else to distraction, so I hide them up here. With me. For a while longer at least. Until they're little more than frail paper. Until they turn to dust at the touch.

If it were up to Mrs Thricefold of course, we'd only ever have permanent botanicals in the house. She claims they're all the rage in Paris. Dearest Biddy. Where would I be without her? She hails from the far flung North. Yorkshire. I very much doubt she even knows where Paris is.

The thing is, she can't be bothered to replace fresh flowers. And her displays are woeful. I caught her massacring the Amaryllis before our guests arrived. And they don't come cheap. When she'd finished they looked like they'd been trampled underfoot during a Boer offensive. But she tries.

GUASTO *smiles. Takes in the rest of the room.*

They remind me of love, you see. Being in love and everything that word means. They should us all. It's why we have them in our homes. We give them to those we cherish. Love. Because love can never last. And we need to be reminded ...What we adore will eventually... sooner or later... be taken... die.

Sorry. I'm making you blush. But you mustn't. Death and love are perfectly natural topics for conversation. And we'll all certainly encounter one of them first hand at some stage in our lives. And spend some considerable time in pursuit of the other... What? You don't strike me as the sort of young man who'd be rendered speechless when confronted by a member of the fairer sex happy to talk freely about emotion. You'll find I'm a very modern woman Mr... sorry it's gone.

GUASTO Guasto.

EDITH You don't sound especially French to me.

GUASTO I come from an old family. Our line began in Italy.

EDITH Foreigners. Such little grace.

GUASTO I'm as English as you are...

EDITH There you go again. We do not constantly correct people in polite society. Everyone's allowed to be wrong. So. Italian heritage. That's the reason for the simmering darkness to your eyes.

GUASTO. I didn't mean to offend Madam Bland...

EDITH I prefer to be called by my pen name. Nesbit. Edith Nesbit. Miss if you must, but I'd rather you'd not. And never Madam or Mrs. I wish there was a term to describe a woman, who neither likes to feel like someone's chattel or overlooked and past her best.

GUASTO I should see how she is...

EDITH Perhaps there will be. One day.

GUASTO The young woman...?

EDITH Guasto? I did study rudimentary Italiana... *(tries to recall the name's meaning)* Guasto...

GUASTO Miss Nesbit?

EDITH She's sleeping quite soundly.

GUASTO The fall she almost took. It could have been nasty.

EDITH But thankfully you caught her. Quite magnificently. So strong...

GUASTO I feel responsible for her.

EDITH Well you're not. We'll send a boy to her parents... The Carrick's you said?

GUASTO They died unfortunately. In terrible circumstances.

Beat.

EDITH Such a nuisance.

GUASTO Truly awful...

EDITH You know the family?

GUASTO No...

EDITH You clearly had a lengthy conversation to be aware of such an intimate tragedy.

GUASTO Not really. Miss Carrick was listening to one of the carols. *Silent Night*. It was clearly upsetting her.

EDITH Odious little tune.

GUASTO She told me about her misfortune almost as soon as we started speaking. I imagine losing loved ones makes Christmas a taxing celebration.

Pause.

EDITH I had wondered who would let a young girl attend our affair alone.

GUASTO Then her fever struck...

EDITH. What that girl is suffering from is a case of bad corsetry. Too tight by far. This miserable season brings out the worst in people. And in girls like her, that means giddiness Mr Guasto. Giddiness. Despite her own private sorrows, she'll have still wanted to impress. Look her best. For the likes of you I dare say. To catch the eye of someone so... Well she wouldn't be able to resist the temptation. I saw her you know. I observed. She was clawing at her clutch bag a little too eagerly...

GUASTO She seems a fragile thing. Delicate.

EDITH She came a cropper due to her own reckless abandon. Well she can stay here until the morning. Then we will find out whoever her legal guardian may be, and I will personally give him a piece of my mind that will ruin his Christmas.

GUASTO That's very charitable of you.

Chimes from somewhere.

EDITH Our guests will be leaving soon. His guests. Every year I suffer this ritual. Hubert insists. He feels it's a socialist's duty to be happy and when is man meant to be happier than at this time of the year. So Thricefold concocts one of her ghastly spiced punches. Hubert drinks too much of it. We have dreary carols. Mince pies that are barely edible. And I get bored. I do. Truly and inconsolably bored.

GUASTO The party seemed like a jolly enough affair to me...

EDITH Forced. I loathe jollity at the best of times. There's something far more honest and safe about melancholy.

The young girl should think herself very lucky. She had a timely escape. And not just from getting her skull cracked on our stairs.

GUASTO In what other way?

EDITH Hubert's monocle was at full tilt in her direction. Almost by the time he'd finished his first jar of punch. I was watching him and that's how I began watching her. He had "set his sights" shall we say. Oh yes. He likes to spread himself about. Always has. I find it hugely amusing. But I'm making you blush again.

EDITH *gets closer to her companion.*

Have you heard the term "sauce for the goose" Mr Guasto? And no. It's not something Thricefold will be ladling from a tureen in a few hours hence.

GUASTO I'm really not sure...

EDITH You're not exactly here by chance are you? Up here with me. *(pause)* Although I pay scant attention to my husband's gatherings, I know for certain the name Guasto wasn't on our invitation list.

GUASTO Well...

EDITH I've already said. I'm a very modern woman.

GUASTO And I'm a huge fan.

Pause.

EDITH Christ! One of them. Might have known.

GUASTO You must hear it all the time...

EDITH I make a point of avoiding fans like one might avoid a dose of *Poe's Red Death*.

GUASTO I had an ailing sister. We didn't hold out much hope for her to begin with, to be honest. But I swear what helped her survive her malady were my readings. *The Railway Children*? *The Phoenix and the Carpet*...?

EDITH Well... there we go... always a pleasure to know I've helped a child live.

GUASTO I adored the stories too. They're enchanting. Although when I first read them...

EDITH You thought the E stood for Edgar or Eugene...

GUASTO How did you know...?

EDITH That is something I may have heard once or twice before...

GUASTO It's a miracle to be here.

EDITH Well it's meant to be the season for them...

GUASTO I've taken rooms on Wicklow Lane two streets...

EDITH I'm well aware of the geography of my home town...

GUASTO My landlady has all your books. First editions housed in grand glass cabinets.

EDITH Maybe she'd like a few more...

EDITH knocks a pile of books to the ground in frustration.

GUASTO We started talking about you, Mrs Fairthought and I, and when she said you actually lived so very close, well...

EDITH You decided to trespass.

GUASTO No...

EDITH What else would you call it?

GUASTO Well not in a way that would mean any harm.

EDITH My feelings for my husband may at times teeter slightly over the brink of loathing but he will still defend me. You may have read of his assault on HG Wells. Punched him in Paddington. Without a qualm.

GUASTO I am here only because of my fascination with you. I'm not going to harm you.

EDITH Of course Wells had dishonoured our daughter at the time. And I've been tempted to strike the swine myself. He will persist on calling me Evelyn. "Dear Evelyn" …Makes me sound like someone's grandmother. But I always manage to restrain myself. Bland's temper often makes him look ridiculous. It used to charm me. He blames the smallpox. Which he's had twice. Men like to blame anything but themselves. Are you like that?

GUASTO I assure you. I am entirely honourable.

EDITH Being *entirely* honourable is dull Mr Guasto. And potentially disappointing.

Pause.

So tell me how you come to be here. What subterfuge did you employ?

GUASTO I'm here, I suppose, because you smiled in my direction.

EDITH I'm sure I'd remember you.

GUASTO The party was beginning and only a handful of your guests were gathered in the hallway. I was on my way home and saw the chance to slide in unseen with the carollers. So I took it. Couldn't resist. Just a glimpse of you, I said to myself, and then I'd slip away again. Like I'd never been here. Then came your smile. It reassured me so I decided to stay a while longer.

Next thing I knew I was talking to the young lady who was alone and a little lost... and... you know the rest

Pause.

EDITH So what do you want?

GUASTO Only the chance to express my admiration for your words. The wonderful worlds you have created. My gratitude.

EDITH Well you've achieved that.

> EDITH *tugs at a velvet chord. She's ringing for Thricefold.*

GUASTO And so much more. I never dreamt I'd get to see your writing room too. The space where you create.

EDITH And where I hide. Though often they are the same thing. Thricefold will be on her way. She'll see you out.

He glances towards the other room.

GUASTO I'd rather not leave. Not yet.

EDITH You're still bleating on about your precious girl?

GUASTO I'm concerned. It's a gentleman's prerogative...

EDITH If her condition worsens, which it won't, we shall send for medical assistance. We are not stupid people. There's even a few doctors downstairs who could well be sober by dawn. Dr Watkins frequently awakens under the pianola on Christmas morning. Although he was struck off when Victoria had pigtails. Ancient. Maybe this Christmas morning he won't wake up at all and he'll still be under the wretched pianola come New Year. Nobody plays it.

> EDITH *laughs.*

GUASTO You seem to find death amusing.

EDITH Of course. It's by far the greatest joke of the lot. Don't you think?

GUASTO Please. I wish to sit here and keep a silent vigil... that is all I ask...

Pause.

EDITH You do want something else. Don't you?

Pause.

GUASTO Now you come to ask yes. Yes I do. But I hardly dare...

Shades of EDITH *the temptress return.*

EDITH Go on.

Pause.

GUASTO A reading.

EDITH But of course!

GUASTO A paragraph. Less. A few lines. Any portion, however meagre, of your well-honed words will suffice.

EDITH I should have bloody well known...

GUASTO It'd be an experience I'd treasure...

EDITH *is struck by an idea.*

EDITH Fine. I hate it when men begin to beg. It's always ungainly. I will do as you ask. You shall have your reading.

GUASTO This is such a tremendous honour...

The lights flicker. GUASTO *is startled.*

EDITH You're the nervous type? The lighting does that the further you climb up this rickety old house. Especially when the lamps are ablaze in every room below, like tonight.

GUASTO May I request a favourite sequence?

EDITH Let me guess. *Five Children and It...*

GUASTO No... I'm unnerved by the creature they find. The eponymous it.

EDITH That's the point.

GUASTO I choose *The Railway Children...*?

EDITH *(in)* I won't be reading from one of my tales for children. Not tonight. If truth be told I can't abide them at the moment. I really can't. So if you want your reading it's on my terms.

GUASTO *is mildly taken aback.*

GUASTO That would be more than acceptable...

EDITH Are you sure? The reading will be from my early works. My first stories. They're not for the faint hearted. I find myself turning back to them more and more these days. The new century was meant to bring with it so much hope. But it's only succeeded in rekindling my acquaintance with darkness and foreboding. Which I will admit is proving to be strangely comforting at times. But mostly Mr Guasto it is deeply unsettling. There are worrying times ahead. I can feel it.

GUASTO I'm not sure I understand...

EDITH The intent of these tales is to terrify. You want to hear me read? Well the price you'll pay is feeling the chill to the very marrow of your bones Mr Guasto.

GUASTO Ghost stories?

EDITH *has found a large book.*

EDITH I leave the ghost stories to others with slighter flair and more prosaic imaginative skills. Take silly Professor James for instance. Who's scared of a billowing sheet, a few old relics or an off tune whistle? Mind, I'm sure they served his purposes. Inspired many of his fey young male students to leap a quiver into his waiting arms. But they're tame and trite. Mine aren't.

A wind howls outside as the lights flicker again.

So are you prepared to have a sleepless night?

GUASTO I don't imagine I have any say in the matter.

EDITH Shall I begin to read?

GUASTO I will admit one thing... I do have a fear of the grave.

EDITH Then my stories will serve a valuable purpose. Think of them as bite sized dress rehearsals for your own impending demise.

GUASTO Perhaps it would be best if we forgot my request...

EDITH You aren't going to let me down...?

GUASTO These stories can't really be suitable for Christmas?

EDITH Oh but they are. In the days before the New Year dawns and the old wanes and weakens, humanity is exceptionally vulnerable to all manner of evil spirit. Did your mother teach you anything?

Reading tales of the supernatural preferably out loud and in a room where the shadows are deep helps mere mortals prepare for the worst. We need to keep our wits sharp and our senses attuned. Be aware of what might be behind us, beyond our imagination and just out of sight. Listen for half heard strange whispers, the creaks and groans hitherto unheard in your abode, loud noises and the sudden arrival of strangers.

Very loud bang as **BIDDY THRICEFOLD** *bursts into the room.* **EDITH** *and* **GUASTO** *react.* **BIDDY** *holds a tray with two cups.*

Thricefold!

BIDDY What? You called for me. I was already on my way up, as it happens. I was worried about that young lass. I saw her eyes glaze over from across the hallway. Like she saw something dreadful. Then down she went.

EDITH Miss Carrick is sleeping.

BIDDY Carrick she's called eh? Carrick?

BIDDY *sits and starts drinking from one of the cups.*

EDITH As thrilled as I always am Biddy, to see you make yourself as comfortable as you please...

BIDDY Season's cheers Mistress! All the very best. You want me to check on her?

EDITH Miss Carrick is not the first girl to faint underneath the mistletoe and she won't be the last.

BIDDY Carrick? You know for a moment before she went, she reminded me of someone. Trick of the light.

Takes another drink.

EDITH Or the spiced punch.

BIDDY Look at me forgetting meself.

EDITH For a change.

BIDDY This was meant for the poor lass. This other one's for you dear. I hate to think of you missing all the fun downstairs. You and your big heart. Your charitable ways.

EDITH I've been planning some fun of my own Biddy.

BIDDY You have?

EDITH What do you think to tales of the uncanny?

BIDDY Oooh I love them. A good murder always tickles me fancy. And as for spirits... whether they're to inebriate or send shivers down the spine, I relish them both. Well you get to my age and nothing scares you more than real life. And the thrills are few and far between of any description. I've had encounters of me own you know... You said she was called Miss Carrick?

EDITH Would you care to join me Biddy whilst I read a few tales to disturb.

BIDDY Would I not!

EDITH These are penned by my own fair hand. And I should warn you, they're brutal.

BIDDY You're a clever lass. You are. And I could do with a rest. And I should be here anyway, shouldn't I? In case missy through there wakes up.

EDITH Then turn the gaslight low.

BIDDY goes to do as she's told. Notices the vases of dead flowers.

BIDDY I threw these dead things...

EDITH You did.

Pause.

BIDDY Oh Edith love... Why do you insist on keeping them...

EDITH You'll leave them be.

BIDDY It's not healthy. How many times...

EDITH Are you asking to be banished to your basement?

BIDDY As you wish. But you know me. I won't hold my tongue if I think my words will help.

EDITH Biddy!

BIDDY *continues to turn down the gas lights.*
EDITH *turns to* **GUASTO**.

Now. Join me in the dark.

BIDDY Hold your horses Mistress. Don't start 'till I'm settled. I must say Mr Thricefold wouldn't approve of me indulging in this sort of an entertainment. And on a Holy Night too. He'll be spinning in his grave. I don't know where this grave of is, of course. But for pities sake, the wicked blighter must be under the sod by now.

Indicates the other cup. **EDITH** *shakes her head not wanting it.*

Don't mind if I do then.

BIDDY *slurps it back. Midnight starts to strike.*

EDITH If we're ready?

BIDDY *and* **GUASTO** *nod.* **BIDDY** *chuckles.* **GUASTO** *is unsettled. The lighting hones in on* **EDITH** *holding her book open.* Carol of the Bells *begins to play.*

Perfect timing. The most dangerous witching hour of the year chimes. It's Christmas morning. And so we begin our tales of sheer malice with hideous happenings, twisted monsters, cruel villains, death and destruction. All crammed to the edge of the page with blood and guts and unhappy endings. Edith Nesbit's *Tales of Terror.*

Scene Two

EDITH John Charrington's Wedding...

EDITH *begins by reading from her book.*

No one ever thought that May Foster would marry John Charrington; but he thought differently. He asked her to marry him before he went up to work in Oxford. She laughed and refused him. He asked her next time he was home. Again she laughed and tossed back her blond hair. The third time he asked she laughed even harder. She said it was becoming a confirmed habit. Although she secretly admired him. And what was not to admire. He was young but worldly wise, dark haired and in possession of noble features, mysteriously good looking.

She holds her hand out to John who joins her.

He was so very full of life and hope, and had prospects so bright they glistened even in the dead of night. John lived by a golden rule. When he wanted something he was resolutely determined to get it.

She takes **GUASTO***'s hand and places it on the open page he takes the book and becomes John Charrington. This will be repeated each time a new story starts...*

GUASTO John was a man of independent means. Left alone in the world having lost his family suddenly as a child. A terrible accident in which he alone survived. He valued every second of his existence and despite having humble beginnings and simple schooling became self-educated, well versed in the ways of the world and a firmly established a fine career. But he was now ready to settle down and continue his family line.

He starts speaking as John.

May will be mine. As all who know me are aware... things which John Charrington intend should happen, have a way of happening!

So finally my dearest May did me the honour. She agreed damn it. She said yes to me.

EDITH *plays the unnamed Best Man, narrator of the tale.*

EDITH Well get me a one way ticket to the end of Nowhere! Charrington how did you do it? *(to audience)* May Foster, sweetheart of our little hamlet, was renowned for being the prettiest girl in a twenty mile radius. We had all set our sights on her. *(darkly)* Some of us had even taken this one step further...

GUASTO I have the devil's luck as well you know dear friend. And, as I'm sure you also know, the devil... charming fellow... always looks after his own.

BIDDY *has become the old retainer Cobbs...*

BIDDY The way I hears it you had to ask for her pretty little dimpled mitt in marriage more than once.

GUASTO But glance at her wry smile next time she passes by, Cobbs you bitter old dog? She's blissfully happy. She wanted me all along. Only her deliciously feisty pride held her back.

BIDDY Blight on your turnip sack. I prey you'll be snarked by a rat catcher's gimple.

GUASTO You are the rat catcher in these parts Cobbs.

BIDDY So I knows what I'm cussing about. And how to carry out the cuss…

EDITH I must say I'm with Cobbs old man. You bewitched our May.

BIDDY Bet he got her to muddle him a love potion using gripes, grubs and bindweed.

EDITH Probably paid a coin or two to Naggerty Nell from under Tweaks Bridge.

BIDDY Last time I visited Naggerty Nell all I got was a vicious scratching in the nether parts. It still hasn't entirely ceased.

GUASTO claps EDITH on the shoulder.

GUASTO I'd suggest you shrug off the envy old chap.

Beat.

EDITH I do it in jest John. That's all. Jest.

GUASTO Good. Because you have a part to play in my wedding. As an only child and an orphan of the parish, you and your kin were my family. You, my one good true friend, will be my best man.

Pause.

EDITH I'd be honoured.

They shake on it.

BIDDY I'll miss the flirting now she's got an intended. My fair May. Though if my own pickled wife had ever found out… I should be glad temptations out of harm's way.

GUASTO Well that's a certainty Cobbs. We've already set the date and it's less than a week away. I love May Foster. Even death wouldn't stop me from marrying her. From making her mine.

John strides off with a flourish.

EDITH Even death...

BIDDY Happen I should be winding my way too. It's Mrs Cobbs fabled crows gizzard gruel for supper. Suddenly the word death has an appealing chime to it...

EDITH I knew how serious Charrington's feelings were. How deep rooted they ran. I'd witnessed him proclaim his vow of love after life to May Foster with my very own eyes.

It was late one night in the graveyard. I had been taking my midnight constitutional to calm my turbulent soul, when I saw the lovebirds sitting before the largest lichen covered head stone near the Charrington family crypt. They toasted each other by sipping saloop, hot, from a copper flask. I knew Charrington's family recipe involved only the rarest of exotic orchids, which now in his prosperity he could afford. My envy smouldered.

Music. **GUASTO** *sits before an unseen May holding a small goblet.*

GUASTO I will love and cherish you May Foster. Dearly, honestly and truly forever and a day. I will adore you in this world and the next. Even death would not prevent me from making you my bride!

EDITH And my own fair heart broke. In two. For I knew in that very moment I'd lost her to him. Truly lost her. I'll confess this now. She had been the love of my life. That most wretched of desires. An illicit night aside laughed off as an unfortunate lapse. My ardour had remained unrequited... So as I watched the pair kiss tenderly, I wept alone hidden in the murky shadows beneath the angrily tangled branches of a petrified rowan...

BIDDY Queer place for wooing. A graveyard. Always knew young Charrington weren't right in the noggin. Mind.

Me and Mrs Cobbs met on the Sewage Works outing. To Clacton. If ever there were an ill-fated omen...

EDITH The wedding plans were formed in haste. A calf picked and slaughtered to be hung for the feast. Posies of viola's and ivy plucked, pruned and arranged. Hymns and sacred verse chosen and rehearsed while bridesmaids got the vapours all hoping next it would be their turn. And I embarked on penning a best man's speech swallowing down bile with each and every platitude I scratched onto the parchment.

Why the rush Charrington old chap? Surely a lengthy courtship is a thing to be relished.

GUASTO I won't wait for my wedding night. I simply won't. I long to be her first love. I already know I'll be her last.

EDITH But how very little he knew about May Foster... and what she and I had once meant to each other. I'm not a bad man. Truly. But for what I did next I will be tormented for the rest of my days on earth, and much longer beyond.

Music stops. The sound of a bike bell.

BIDDY There's a telegram arrived for you young Mr Charrington.

EDITH *(aside)* In our under populated hamlet the rat catcher often doubled as post master.

BIDDY What's wrong John? Your pallor's taken a most unhealthy tinge. Why you've gone as swallow as a donkey with the droop.

GUASTO Dreadful news from Oxford. Mr Batchfig my benefactor has been struck by the typhus on his travels East. His housekeeper fears the light will be snuffed out in mere hours.

BIDDY Put that out your mind. He'd understand in the circumstance. Your wedding to May is tomorrow at noon...

EDITH But Batchfig has been like a father to you.

GUASTO He has.

EDITH Bad luck old fellow. That such a significant final farewell should collide with the forging of your blissful future.

BIDDY Remember the old man as he was.

EDITH But nevertheless, it's certain your dear Batchfig's dying wish will be to see you once more.

Pause.

GUASTO You're right. I can't let him die alone. I must head to Oxford on the very next train.

BIDDY But May will be in a dreadful state.

GUASTO It's the eve of our wedding, the one night we can't be together before we're together forever. I'll take my mourning suit and she need never know.

BIDDY What if you don't make it back...?

EDITH But Charrington had already hailed a carriage and had started on his mission of mercy.

And what if he didn't make it back? Even in a situation such as this, a matter of life and death, a jilted bride is still a jilted bride. And who would the bereft May turn to, in her state of shame, in her hour of dire need?

Music for passage of time.

Dawn. The morning of John Charrington's wedding. He hadn't arrived home during the night. My plans were falling neatly into place. This time the devil was backing me.

The sound of a bike bell.

BIDDY Another telegram. Batchfig carked it at midnight. Charrington's heading for the first train out of Oxford. We're to collect him.

EDITH I went with Cobbs, my thudding heart heavy as a mortuary slab. I couldn't believe it. He'd beaten all odds and won again.

BIDDY and EDITH upend a trunk and sit on it as if it were a carriage. BIDDY has the reigns.

BIDDY There's the Oxford Express chugging in to platform three. Bang on time as per. If there's one thing you can trust it's our Great British trains. And long may that continue... We'll get the lad dandied up with spittle and smudgings, an he'll be at the church in the nick of time.

EDITH But to my glee as the last passenger left the station, there was no sign of John Charrington.

BIDDY Lordy. Well this is a mug boggle and a quart. As they say where I'm from... Charrington's buggered.

EDITH To the church Cobbs. No time to delay

BIDDY and EDITH bounce furiously as if travelling in haste.

"We must do all we can to save May Fosters shame" I instructed Cobbs. "We needed to get her well away from the alter before she even has an inkling that her betrothed has let her down."

And then she would, given time and gentle nurturing, be mine all mine once again.

The church bells peel.

BIDDY Well I'll be bladder whacked by a mutt snap. Somehow the service has started.

EDITH And the discordant piping of the ancient church organ suggested it was well underway. I hastily collared a cleric. The groom was in attendance... had been for an age before anyone else turned up in fact. Had he played me for a fool..?

BIDDY He must have arrived by other means.

EDITH Cobbs entered the church and I followed furiously behind, trying not to curse but kicking the font on my way with the might of all my pent up spite.

Things get darker as we enter the church. And scarier. Unsettling organ music. **GUASTO** *stands with his back to the audience. Something is clearly wrong with the groom... He turns slowly and looks like the dead... which in fact he is.*

John. My good friend John. My brother in all but blood. We feared you had missed the train. Worried you'd miss this joyous day.

GUASTO *glares at* **EDITH**. **BIDDY** *throws a handful of black confetti.*

BIDDY Quick after him! There's something afoot, the new Mrs Charrington looks like she's seen a demon from the very pits of Hell. I'd help give chase but Mrs Cobbs has stumbled and is wedged betwixt two pews.

EDITH I fled the church with others who also had decided something strange had just taken place. Charrington took his Bride into an awaiting coach pulled by black plumed stallions. It sped away almost as if the beasts hooves were taking flight. And I recalled Charrington's promise. Even death wouldn't prevent him marrying May Foster. What grisly supernatural happening had I been the architect of?

Bike ring.

BIDDY   And another telegram. Terrible news. And impossible. I didn't see this coming! Charrington perished quite violently in a carriage calamity whilst heading home on the way to Oxford station. But how…

EDITH   Not even death.

BIDDY   We found poor May in the graveyard.

EDITH   In the exact same spot where I'd watched her with her husband to be…

BIDDY   The autumn sun set swiftly that night as we stood in the stillness. Not a bit of breeze to the air. But a dread cold. Unnatural.

EDITH   My darling?

BIDDY   Why's she lying face down? She'll stain her lovely dress.

EDITH   My one true darling.

BIDDY   And she's so still. I'd stand back. Leave her be the poor lamb.

EDITH   But she's safe now.

BIDDY   Have you lost your sense? Something aint right.

EDITH   Safe from whatever became of Charrington. Whatever monstrous happening twisted his soul…

BIDDY   Unnatural I tell you. And that buzzing. A sound I know all too well. It's the flies feasting on something long dead… I smell something rotten…

EDITH   It was me my darling.

BIDDY   It's coming from…

EDITH   I was the one you were meant to share your life with. Your life.

BIDDY   Don't turn her over.

EDITH I did all I could to make fate find a different path. For us. I did it for us...

BIDDY I said don't.

> **EDITH** *does. Both she and* **BIDDY** *confront the horror of May's remains as the music reaches a crescendo.*

> **EDITH** *once again reads from the book.*

EDITH Death had come for May. Hard. Took her beauty. Her soul. And what little was left of the wretched remnants of mine. What had passed in the carriage on that devilish drive? No one knows. No one would ever know.

But John Charrington was always a man of his word.

> *As the lights flicker back up the players are themselves once more...*

GUASTO Stop!

Scene Three

We're back in the attic. **BIDDY**'s *nodded off.*

EDITH What? That was a happy ending.

GUASTO Happy?

EDITH Bride and groom took their place side by side in the Charrington crypt dressed in their wedding finery. All be it soiled in places from putrification.

GUASTO And the narrator.

EDITH He'd have a long life. Spent alone, learning that there are indeed fates worse than death.

GUASTO You didn't need to kill her...

EDITH Where would be the fun if she survived?

GUASTO Women shouldn't think of such cruelty.

EDITH Are your opinions so superficial you think we're not capable of cruelty?

GUASTO No.

EDITH I'm pleased to hear it. A writer's role regardless of gender, is to give an impression of reality. Their version. Even if her work belongs in the realms of the fantastic it has to be real in some way. People do encounter barbarous twists of fate. They can die well before their time.

BIDDY *awakens.*

May's fate was entwined inexorably in her husbands. Isn't that as the law would have it? Isn't that how it is in the eyes of God? For better or worse. Well in my opinion May skipped the worse bit by being snuffed out before her marriage flourished. Before she got to spend decade after decade living a life in which love and desire turned to familiarity and habit and deceit and disdain. Trapped there by an abhorrent and archaic ritual that if I had my way...

BIDDY Listen to you banging on again.

EDITH Back in the land of the living I see.

BIDDY You saying I've been asleep. I never have. I was mulling over the plot and I don't care a pennorth for your opinions. In my eyes that story was ever so romantic. Warmed my fluttering heart. It did!

EDITH *(snappy)* It's not meant to, you odd old woman. And besides... the punch got the better of you long before the climax.

BIDDY I got the gist. Look what handsome Mr Charrington went through for the love of doomed little May. The odd infestation aside, the most Mr Thricefold ever did for me was help slacken a gammy tooth with a second hand dolly stick. You should've seen the shock on his chops when I hit the bugger back. Ha! Last time I clapped eyes on his worthless carcass he still had a touch of hobble to his step.

GUASTO *(quietly)* Wouldn't he have had pity on her? He loved her.

EDITH Life can be grim. And violent.

BIDDY A trip down Sparrows Lane on Sheep Market Day's enough to remind you that. Let's have another story.

EDITH Are you certain?

BIDDY I've got the taste.

She drains her mug. **EDITH** *turns to* **GUASTO** *who won't look at her.*

EDITH What shall it be??

GUASTO Where does it come from? Why did you feel the need to write of such abomination...

EDITH looks through her book. *BIDDY starts nodding off again.*

EDITH My inspirations are varied. I see the darkness in almost everything.

GUASTO A curse...

EDITH You may think so.

GUASTO Are your other tales as terrible?

EDITH Of course. And clever... *Take The Violet Car* for example. It involves an aged servant girl come nurse becoming entangled in a miasma of unpleasantness that could be down to the failing of her own mental faculties or something far sinister. When I wrote it Biddy hadn't long been with us.

BIDDY What was that?

EDITH I'm trying to decide which story to read next dear.

BIDDY Something with a bit more gore. That'll get my circulation going.

GUASTO Please... I'd rather we simply chatted...

EDITH *Man Sized in Marble!* In which two monstrous statues awaken at midnight, intent on gratuitous destruction.

GUASTO I've heard enough.

EDITH A gormless new wife gets her skull crushed to pulp for no other reason than the notion entertained me.

BIDDY Read that one in an old penny dreadful. Ever so lurid.

EDITH turns to GUASTO who won't look at her.

EDITH I fear it may be too distressing??

But this? The very thing.

I like to make the terrors I unveil unique and original. I see little sense in exercising the imagination if you're going to re-tread the same tired path. But enough of poor syphilitic Mr Bram Stoker...

Music.

Scene Four

EDITH A tale of rivalry, greed and social altercation featuring the eerie and sensational evil of a most singular horror. I present...

The Pavilion.

Amelia Davenant was an heiress of renown. As well a one of those charmless and featureless blondes the wrong side of pretty. The wrong side of dainty. The wrong side of loveable.

EDITH *looks between* BIDDY *and* GUASTO. *She sets her sight on* GUASTO. *Holds out her hand. He tries to look away. Beat. He gets up and as before allows his hand to be placed on the book and reads.*

GUASTO Amelia had wealth, an estate and a permanent sense of foreboding. She knew her beloved parents would all too soon be making worms fat. She also knew when the inevitable occurred all she'd have was her land, her servants and several corridors worth of desolate empty rooms. No wit. No wisdom. Nowhere-for all. Nothing else.

GUASTO *becomes Amelia.*

I, Amelia Davenant, you see, was one of those forlorn creatures who seem born to be left far behind and alone. But one person kept my spirits sparkling. I had a dear delightful lifelong friend.

EDITH *becomes Ernestine.*

EDITH Ernestine Pertspank. Of the Pilbury Pertspanks?... surely you know of us? Everyone does... a long and noble but fecklessly destitute line of landed gentry. Many people asked why I was so close to the dull but fabulously rich and deeply generous Amelia. My swollen good heart of course. I was the very best friend a girl could have.

For although far prettier, more prone to whimsy and in possession of many other enchanting and winning ways... I still realised one thing. Poor lumpen unattractive people like Amelia were still people. They needed friends too. However tiresome being the friend of a person with the grace of one of their father's livestock... could be.

GUASTO As an aside. I feel I should confess, much as I loved my wincingly sweet, darling friend Ernestine, there were times when her smile, perfect dress sense and never a lock of stray hair... made me positively gaseous. With despair as well as disgust.

EDITH Oh Amelia. I'm exhausted. This dance has made my alacrity shrivel with its rigor. But I have no more availability. When my vigour is replenished I have no space. Crammed I tell you. To the very brim. May I borrow your dance card? Dear friend?

GUASTO I'm still actively engaged in attracting the attention of dashing young men with it dear friend. Move along...

EDITH Pretty Please? You always have ample room on yours. Pages and pages and pages.

Pause.

GUASTO She had no idea how her well-intended words could wound.

EDITH Although at times a twinkle to her eye suggested otherwise. Come Amelia there's a strident colonel I'd like to meet. And dear friend, I always look my very best with you at my side.

GUASTO I knew that was an insult but smiled graciously. As was my way.

BIDDY *becomes Colonel Batlock.*

BIDDY Davenant Hall's annual Winter Ball was a tradition in these parts much lauded and discussed for months before and after. Well this season it would be bigger and better than ever before. I was there. Colonel Sandford Batlock fresh from tackling the Dutch and decorated to within an inch of my life. Lots of blood on these hands. Increases the appeal. The swoon factor soars when the fillies here about death. I was quite the catch in several territories. And for this special occasion I'd let it be known my days at war were won and done. I was searching for a bride. And a bride like the Davenant's daughter may come with added fiscal perks.

GUASTO And here I am Colonel Batlock. Amelia Davenant. Would you care to dance?

BIDDY Good Lord...

GUASTO I may be able to fit you in. I do believe they're tuning up for a Mazurka...

EDITH *steps in.*

EDITH Colonel your medals... my how they dazzle a girl's eyes.

BIDDY Likewise your smile is doing exactly the same to me...

EDITH Ernestine Pertspank. I think you should have your first dance with me...

BIDDY *addresses the audience.*

BIDDY A dilemma. Although it may seem obvious to the casual viewer which maiden to woo, I have a brace of closely guarded secrets. Firstly I never triumphed in the Transvaal. Wouldn't know a blundering Boer from a Zulu dawn. The medals are pilfered. The title's concocted. Secondly, I'm pitifully broke with debts to pay. Down at heel. Miss Davenant's dowry is known to be as abundant as Miss Pertspank's... spirit.

GUASTO My parents added heftily to my dowry each year.

EDITH But despite this. The dance card remained... un-besmirched by even a trickle of ink.

GUASTO Trollop.

EDITH Frump.

BIDDY Ladies, ladies. They're playing the *Dashing White Sergeant* and I'm afraid my war wounds won't permit rigorous jigging.

GUASTO Poor brave you.

EDITH *mimes vomiting.*

BIDDY Avarice got the better of me... as is my want... I will dance with you in time my delicate sweet Ernestina. But for now dear... fulsome Amelia.

GUASTO He called me fulsome everybody!

BIDDY Shall we, Amelia, take a stroll around this glorious estate? The weather is mild for the time of year.

GUASTO At last. I was in my element.

EDITH But not for long.

Music. They "move outdoors".

GUASTO We walked far from the hall in the direction of an abandoned pavilion locked up for the season.

EDITH I followed unseen.

GUASTO Or so she thought. I was all eyes when it came to that spite raddled harpy and her corsets trussed to her spindly ribs within an inch of her pitiful life. My dear friend.

EDITH I knew the game I was playing all too well. I'd choose my moment and present myself to the colonel in a manner he simply wouldn't be able to resist.

BIDDY *has become the "old retainer" Fret.*

BIDDY I was out that night, the night of the great ball. I loved digging in the dusk. There's always work to be doing when your trade is that of the odd job. And besides I have no time for the fancy affairs of the hall. I was restless.

Oswald Fret's my name. It's my nature too. Though I've worked for the Davenant family four score and umpteen, the land here gives me the shudders.

Plants don't flourish as they should. Not as nature intended. And the fruit they bare... I once dug up a beetroot with eyes... that blinked... So I did. None of the jumbled beggars that work up at the house believe me.

Nor do they believe the ancient oak in the field that yields crops with a tenacious form of blight, can be heard singing devilishly at harvest time. They look at me and say 'Fret away'... and I harbour my secrets alone.

But what of the plant that grows round the pavilion? Even the others, the fools who toil this land, even they pause for concern.

EDITH *and* **GUASTO** *join* **BIDDY** *as gardeners.*

GUASTO Nothing we do rots that weed.

EDITH The faster we cut it, the hardier it thrives. The scythes I've ruined.

GUASTO It's aberrant it is. Sure as my granny suckled baby sheep in last April's blizzard.

BIDDY But I'm the only one who's seen the poison vine bud.

EDITH You never have old Fret...

GUASTO Do tell.

BIDDY I swear it had teeth as near human as anything I ever saw. I swear assure my name is Fret. I swear they smiled at the sight of the old blue veins, still pumping with vitality in my scrawny arms as I reached over them...

EDITH And tonight those vines are terrible restless. Writhing. I swear I saw them writhing.

GUASTO At the every sight of them my stomach's churning like a barrel of rancid buttermilk.

BIDDY So when I saw the young mistress head past me in the direction of the pavilion. Well... I hollered out to her I did. I did my best as befits an employee of a grand old house...

"That's right mistress. The pavillion's lovely this evening. A perfect spot to view the entire estate."

And good luck. Never could stand her.

GUASTO *is Amelia once more.*

GUASTO Of course I ignored the gruntings of the old retainers. When I ruled the hall I'd be shot of the lot. But no time to dwell on future glory tonight. I knew exactly what I was doing. Preparing to teach someone a lesson.

BIDDY *becomes the colonel again.*

BIDDY So all these acres. Fields stretching as far as one can see. This will one day be yours.

GUASTO And mine alone. This old hall, it's many, many out buildings and the fields that stretch as far as the eye can see are a testament to one true fact of life.

Looks to **EDITH**, *who ducks.*

Young looks fade. Old money doesn't.

EDITH That was close. I will hide in this ramshackle shelter and listen to their conversation from its dark recesses. There I will pick my moment to strike with cupid's arrow…

EDITH *vanishes.*

BIDDY Tell me about this old pavilion my dear?

GUASTO Mother and father used to hold affairs in it during midsummer.

BIDDY It's seen better days.

GUASTO It became suddenly and inexplicably, over run with bindweed. Of a quite rampant variety sir.

BIDDY In my time I've studied botany…

GUASTO Brains as well as brawn.

BIDDY Yes indeed. *(aside to audience)* Another lie but I'm on a roll… In all my studies I've never seen a species like it.

GUASTO The way of the plant is strange and unpredictable. We think it's haunted.

BIDDY How can a plant be haunted?

GUASTO There isn't a gardener in the county who could uproot or destroy it. If you look hard enough you can almost see it grow.

An unnerving lighting effect catches **BIDDY**'s *eye.*

BIDDY A strange illusion. A deception caused by the rapidly fading light. That's all.

GUASTO Not only that. Our dog Romeo went missing last year. We found him dead. Right here on this very spot. Curiously there was not a single drop of blood left in his corpse.

BIDDY Wild animals. Such a nuisance in these parts. Maybe we should be heading back.

GUASTO Indeed. Oh look. The pavilion gate has somehow creaked open. I'd better secure it. We have been known to fall foul of vagrancy.

Big slam.

If there's one thing I can't tolerate... It's tramps!

BIDDY *and* **GUASTO** *go.* **EDITH** *emerges.*

EDITH That great galloping guttersnipe. She knew I was here all along and she's locked me in. *(shouts)* Hear me you... narwhale... If I catch even a sniffle or snag the slightest scrap of silky hem...

She stops. So does the plant. She's sure she's seen it move...

That tale she told. Her imagination is all she has. All that time alone. It's taken its toll on far more than her waist line. I pity her, but if she thinks she can scare me she can think again. Haunted weeds. What a load of...

And the plants pounce. Deep terrifying screams as the stage goes black. The gluggling chuckles of a vampire plant.

Time passes.

Lights up on **GUASTO** *as Amelia.*

GUASTO I didn't intend for Ernestina to die. So horribly. I merely wished to teach the strumpet once and for all not to mess with the affairs of my heart. To frighten her and dampen her seemingly indefatigable spirit. But the next day as dawn broke Fret the old retainer found Ernestine at the pavilion. White as a marble sarcophagus. Entirely drained of her life's blood. Such beauty cruelly and hideously extinguished.

Oh well.

Father hushed the whole thing up. He's good like that. And would you believe it. Braggart proposed two days later. The colonel swept me off my feet when I declared "Yes… oh Yes." Well he made an attempt stopped only by a particularly pernicious war wound near his groin. I recovered swiftly from the fall. Mild concussion merely needs a few days in a darkened room after all. And now finally here we are… our wedding night. Mine.

An eerie sound. Is it the name Amelia being called.

I think of her. Ernestina. I miss her. To a fashion. Sometimes I stand and watch the pavilion from the bedroom window. I imagine I see her floating in the shadows… I have too much time on my hands. Braggart has been out a lot lately. Spending the down payment on my dowry. It gives me pleasure to see him happy. But sometimes he doesn't return to the hall for days. And it's lonely here. Soon after my engagement mother fell from her mare on her morning ride. Dead before she knew it. And father went downhill so swiftly my dear Benjamin saw fit to admit him into a sanatorium. I never see him.

Being loved is all that matters. I know that. I have everything I truly need.

An eerie voice sounds "Amelia, Amelia".

Sometimes I dream about her. I wish she were here tonight. I wish deep down I hadn't killed... I hadn't been foolish enough to let my harmless prank go as far... I would dearly love to share my overwhelming joy and happiness with her...

We hear the voice again. EDITH *appears as a ghostly Ernestine clutching an eerie looking Bridal Bouquet.*

EDITH Then let me in to your room my dear.

GUASTO My friend. Ernestina.

EDITH Let me in.

GUASTO I've missed you. I knew you couldn't truly be dead.

EDITH You have to invite me across the threshold.

GUASTO Of course. Come in at once. Please...

EDITH I've brought you this to wish you luck. It's my duty. After all, in the unlikely event of you becoming betrothed whilst I was still on this plane I'm certain I'd have been your bridesmaid.

GUASTO Oh certainly Ernestina. But what are you talking about? You're here now. I can change my arrangements. I can do anything. I'm rich...

EDITH Take the bouquet. I gathered it the night I died.

GUASTO You're obviously not dead...

EDITH It flourishes at the pavilion. It brings with it a gift. A gift of survival.

GUASTO The unfathomable plant? Did you learn its secret?

EDITH And so shall you dear Amelia. The secret of eternal happiness.

GUASTO *takes the plant.*

The secret of the undead.

EDITH *bares her fangs as the bouquet... somehow... reaches up and grabs Amelia. Lights up on* **EDITH**.

And as the depth of night approached Amelia found new life. She and Ernestina were united at last. And their first thoughts were a need to feed. So how fortuitous that at that very moment the Godless would be colonel returned the hall rejoicing that in hours the place would belong to him. He had hoped before Ernestina's demise he would negotiate a compromise. A situation in which he could share both women. But what a twist of fate. For now of course... they were going to share him...

GUASTO *grabs the book... Light change.*

Scene Five

BIDDY *has gone.* **GUASTO** *throws the book down.*

GUASTO I will not listen to any more of this...

EDITH I was getting to the really good bit. The colonel is about to get his just desserts...

GUASTO I don't wish to know the fate that awaits him.

EDITH He deserves to be disembowelled. His particulars eaten whilst still alive. Damn. There you go. That's spoiled the surprise.

GUASTO Will you stop?

A chime.

EDITH Come. There's still time for more...

GUASTO If you insist I can't look in on the young mistress.

EDITH Not her again.

GUASTO I should take my leave.

EDITH Stay. You amuse me. And where's your spirit? Listen. The house is silent. Most of the revellers have gone. Biddy is making certain Miss Carrick remains in absolute comfort... so you don't need to worry on that count.

Come closer. Poor thing. So vulnerable when all is said and done. So earnest and noble and... handsome.

We're alone. Let me offer you something in the way of comfort. Calm your querulous nerves.

GUASTO Mrs Fairthought will lock up the house.

EDITH There isn't a single well to do gentlemen in this part of town who doesn't own a latch key to his lodgings. You're shaking...

GUASTO Violence. I don't like violence. That's all. You kill the young with no reason and no mercy.

EDITH The reason is to teach the reader they need to live to the full while they can. Seize the day. The moment.

EDITH kisses GUASTO. Against his better judgement he responds. When this happens EDITH breaks away suddenly. Music starts.

Why you're cold. Colder than... *(a revelation)* Guasto. Guasto. That's it. I've finally remembered. I know the meaning of your name.

Music. Lights out.

ACT TWO

Scene One

EDITH *sits centre. Light only on her as she reads from* The Railway Children. *The reading is accompanied by vivid sound effects.*

EDITH "Roberta! Roberta! Why look Roberta" cried Peter while a sobbing Phyllis struggled to keep up with her siblings. They bounded along the railway embankment and try as she might her little legs simply weren't up to it.

"See the cloudy billow of steam beyond the hillock?" Peter struggled to catch his breath. "We'll be too late to avert the disaster."

"We can't be too late Peter", Roberta was determined. "We simply can't. We must wave at the driver with all our might using petticoats mother made for us in a deeply inappropriate shade of scarlet.

Peter agreed, not even stopping for an instant to ponder the inappropriate shade of his mother's most personal items of clothing. It was imperative that the train did not turn the bend and hit the landside that had fallen on the track. The children screamed with all their might waving the deep red rags which signalled a terrible warning.

EDITH *stops consulting the book.*

The good news is the steam train didn't collide with the peril that lay in wait. Alas the bad news is at the sight of the maniacal screaming children the driver, fearing his vehicle was about to be beset by demented delinquents, pulled on his breaks with as mighty and tremendous a force the knotted muscles of his meaty arms had ever achieved.

The great steaming engine buckled the tracks beneath its vast wheels before hurtling out of control and spontaneously combusting into flame.

Its path of absolute destruction was heading in the direction of the embankment, where Roberta, Peter and Phyllis, our dear darling Railway Children, stood rooted with pee trickled summer legs in utter abject terror...

The sound of crashing an explosion and children screaming. The lights come up. EDITH *is alone with* GUASTO *who sits before her.*

GUASTO That isn't in the story.

EDITH You don't say. But maybe it would were I to write it now... Mr Dead.

Chimes.

GUASTO I asked you politely not to call me that.

EDITH I'm rarely polite.

GUASTO Our family name has been a burden to us for generations.

EDITH I can't see why. I mean, I married a Bland. Most of the time I wished he lived up to his name.

GUASTO My Great Grandfather was the first to decide to use our Italian heritage to our advantage. We became the Guasto's.

EDITH Interesting. And hilarious. Fancy. being called Dead. I'm amused.

GUASTO It's far from amusing. It's haunted me all of my life.

EDITH You do take yourself very seriously don't you?

Pause.

GUASTO I don't understand. How could someone who's put so much enchantment and magic into so many childhoods...

EDITH I'm a good writer. I'm versatile... And there has always been an appetite for imagined horrors. They made me good money when we needed it most

GUASTO Then why did you stop.

EDITH I'd said everything I wanted to say.

GUASTO And you left your dark side behind.

EDITH Not entirely. Why do you think my children's books are devoured with such an appetite? However fantastical they may be they're real. And they don't shy away from the unpleasant. The wrongful imprisonment of the Railway Children's father. The tragic death of the Bastable's mother. The demise of the beloved Phoenix.

Children are infinitely more intelligent readers than adults.

Beat.

As a child we holidayed in Bordeaux. Father was a stickler for learning and I thank him for that. I've had advantages others of my sex have missed. But even a holiday needed to be educational. We went to the church of Saint Michel. The heat was stifling. The place reeked of decay. I had wanted to leave but it wasn't to be. Not until we saw the crypt.

In this crypt ran a railing. Behind it – standing against the wall with a ghastly look of life in death – were about two hundred skeletons hung on wires. Skeletons with their flesh hardened on their bones, with their long hair hanging on each side of their browned faces where the skin in drying had drawn itself back from their gleaming teeth and empty eye-sockets. As they stood there in their shredded shrouds it was if they were reaching out... The crowning horror of my childish life.

GUASTO But you used this horror as inspiration?

EDITH I had to. I resolved that my own children should never know such fear. I had to purge the memory.

GUASTO So you wrote your stories.

EDITH Yes. An attempt to banish the darkness from my own soul.

GUASTO But darkness never really goes. It waits to seep back in...

Pause. **EDITH** *is unnerved by* **GUASTO**'s *comment.*

EDITH Sit closer to the fire. You're clearly freezing. And growing paler. You're paler than the December moon out there.

GUASTO My body temperature is unusually low. A quirk of nature. A family trait.

EDITH When I kissed you... You have the start of a chill at the very least. And you're worried about Miss Carrick?

GUASTO Look. I need to see her. I know she's in safe hands now but if I saw her I'd still feel better.

EDITH In your state? I think you're in far poorer health than her.

GUASTO I'd merely glance in on her from the doorway. That's all I would need. All it would take...

EDITH Perhaps in a while when some colour returns to your cheek. In the meantime... One more tale...

BIDDY *enters with a jug.*

How is Miss Carrick?

BIDDY She's free of fever and sleeping like a cherub.

EDITH *(to* **GUASTO***)* Has that set your mind to rest ?

GUASTO *nods.*

BIDDY It has indeed. But I worry that her sleep is very deep for a young slip of a girl. I think her ailment may be down to a tad more than the way she trussed herself up.

EDITH I see you also took a second to nip downstairs.

BIDDY Needed to check that dopey Maude and insolent Maidie and had blown out all the candles.

EDITH And to top up supplies of spiced punch.

BIDDY Only to stop Mr Bland polishing the lot off on his tod. I was saving him from himself. And besides. My nerves. I can't handle all these grisly happenings without some form of fortification.

EDITH We're about to resume our reading.

BIDDY Good. You know that young girl's face. I still have a nagging hunch I know her.

EDITH If there's one thing duller than listening to peoples woes, it's listening to their nagging hunches.

BIDDY Or perhaps it's her family I'm acquainted with?

EDITH Especially yours.

BIDDY I know that many people.

EDITH Because you're an interfering old witch. Sit down. You're irritating me.

BIDDY What did you say her name was again?

EDITH Something gentler I feel as we approach the dawn. And to give your nerves a respite. Let me see... here we go – a ghostly love story...

BIDDY Romance. You can keep your romance.

EDITH I'm not talking to you.

> **BIDDY** *opens her mouth to answer but stops herself. She's clearly a bit bemused by* **EDITH**'s *comment.*

Here we are... a ghostly love story.

Scene Two

EDITH The sorrowful story of Uncle Abraham's Romance.

"No no my dears," Abraham would say, "Nothing romantic never happened to me. Look at me? I'm not suited to romance. Not really. I've never been troubled by matters of that nature. Except... well once... I fell in love. I truly believe that's what it was. Love. But thinking back it's hard to say what truly happened that wonderful December... even to this day I'm uncertain. But I swear it. I swear I lost my heart"...

EDITH *holds her hand out to* BIDDY *who joins her.*

BIDDY He was known to the local children as Uncle Abraham. The harmless lame organ grinder who played his box of music in all weathers and seasons without a complaint. His job was to entertain. And he'd never be accused of not fulfilling his duties.

Music. Christmas music played by a creepy street organ. BIDDY *becomes Abraham.*

Penny for a song my dears? It's Christmas and a song's so good for the soul. And it brings you good luck. Worth it. You also get the chance to see Figaro my monkey dance as I play. He's one for the ladies. Throw him a peanut madam if you wish...

That's right Figaro. That's my good boy.

The sound of young girls laughing at him.

I know what youth means. And love and happiness. Look at me... come on look hard. See what I'm thinking. Here… see me now as a young sapling…there I am… bonny but half witted. What I didn't know…

GUASTO *becomes the young Abraham.*

GUASTO I was always lame and the girls used to laugh at me.

BIDDY I was ever so lonely. Still would be today if I'd not learned how to live with it. Back then…

GUASTO …I got into the way of mooning off by myself to lonely places. One of my favourite walks was up through our churchyard, which was set on a hill in the middle of a marsh.

BIDDY It was December. I'd watched the winter sun set and a white full moon plump and ripe take its place in the centre of a starry sky. And she was there.

EDITH *sits on a gravestone as Susannah.*

EDITH Back again boy.

GUASTO She was sat dressed in her best and seemed to take no heed of the late hour nor the carpet of frost that surrounded her.

EDITH I know you.

GUASTO You do Miss?

EDITH I see you. And watch you. Now and then. My woebegone boy. That's what I call you.

GUASTO You do?

EDITH You're so wistful. It's in the slowness of your step. Your eyes so brilliantly blue but without lustre. You're lonely.

GUASTO I don't mind so much miss. I'm content enough.

EDITH But still… ever so lonely.

GUASTO Happy in my own way.

EDITH I'm lonely too.

GUASTO That's a shame miss.

EDITH I often take my place here in the moonlight when I'm at my loneliest. By the yew tree. I find it restful. And romantic...

GUASTO Yes miss...

BIDDY I didn't know where to look.

GUASTO I'd better carry on with my walking.

EDITH If you must you must...

BIDDY If I'd had any spark of imagination in my bashful noggin I'd have asked her to walk with me.

GUASTO But she wasn't wearing shoes. And in this fearfully cold weather! My very breath froze and swirled like misty angels round my head.

EDITH Sweet boy. You're ever so sweet.

BIDDY I returned night after night that week and she was always there. Like she was waiting for me. Why would she wait for me? Nobody had before. Nobody would again. I never knew her name. Not then...

GUASTO But I had names enough in my heart to call her by.

We hear the music of the street organ but fainter.

EDITH Listen boy... the sound of the Christmas Fair. How I love the sound of a street organ. How it fills my spirits. Do you dance?

GUASTO Me miss. No miss. I can't...

EDITH Of course not. How I wish I could have one last dance before the moon wanes. I will be leaving soon.

GUASTO You will miss?

EDITH Leaving you.

GUASTO That's a pity, that is.

BIDDY Kiss her you fool.

EDITH But I suspect you'd like to see me again.

> **GUASTO** *shrugs.*

BIDDY Yes! Say yes!

> **GUASTO** *opens his mouth as if to speak… but can't find the words.*

EDITH If you come back in the New Year before the new moon, I shall meet you here just as usual. But if the new moon shines on this grave and you aren't here, you will never see me again.

BIDDY Then she stood. Rose like she was flying. Elegant. Graceful. Were her feet even touching the ground? I saw the inscription on the tomb where she perched. It read Susannah Kingsnorth 1723…

EDITH Don't forget me my woebegone boy.

GUASTO I'll be here miss. Fear not. I will. Of that you can be certain.

BIDDY I spent that Christmas with kinsfolk. A wizened aunt called Cherish and her daughter Mags, who believed in prayer and little else.

GUASTO On their gnarled black wood sideboard sat a small painting. I noticed it on Christmas Day as I choked back parched poultry in the silent dust of the dining room.

> **BIDDY** *becomes Aunt Cherish* **EDITH** *becomes Mags…*

EDITH She's caught your eye.

BIDDY Taken a liking to the lass? The painting captures her well. Does her fabled looks justice.

EDITH She was one of ours. In the family a generation or so ago.

BIDDY Beloved by boys across the county and beyond.

EDITH Not one of them half-witted like you.

BIDDY Betrothed finally to a wealthy man because why not. She had her pick. Would have married well. But died before the wedding bless her soul.

EDITH Crushed without her shoes on

BIDDY At the Christmas fair by a street organ.

EDITH They say the grinder was afflicted.

BIDDY The demon drink.

EDITH That's men folk for you.

BIDDY Tragic.

EDITH Indeed Mother Cherish. Tragic.

BIDDY But when all is said and done Mags my girl, that's what you get for dancing bare foot on a holy week.

EDITH They said she had the spark of a witch to her. But pretty isn't she? Can you see the family likeness? Her name's on the back.

BIDDY Susannah Kingsnorth.

GUASTO A second. That's all it took for the name to sink in. Suddenly the heat in the room was stifling. I felt as if my breath was being sucked out of my body by an unseen and terrible power...

BIDDY I fell into a fevered shock and was bedridden for days. When the fever broke. It was too late.

GUASTO I missed the new moon. How could I. I missed her. I'd have gone to the ends of the earth with her. The ends of the earth and beyond. But now I knew. As she'd warned me. I'd never see Susannah again.

Music as **GUASTO** *weeps for his lost love.*

BIDDY Come on then Figaro. More revellers on the way. More songs to play and pennies to earn. Let's grind the organ. Grind it slowly. Grind and grind again.

I'm content enough. Happy in my own way.

But sometimes I wonder. Every time December comes. What if I had seen my love again. Would she have taught me to dance at last?

EDITH *and* **GUASTO** *dance to the music.*

I know what youth means, and love and happiness, though I was always lame and the girls used to laugh at me.

The music builds.

EDITH Poor Uncle Abraham. That very Christmas he was found quite frozen. Lying in the graveyard. On the grave of Susannah Kingnorth.

Scene Three

BIDDY's lost in thought as EDITH snaps her book shut.

EDITH You see. Sometimes I can write from the heart.

GUASTO I don't understand. If you wrote these stories to purge your soul why have you returned to them.

BIDDY Wait a minute.

EDITH I didn't know they were a premonition.

BIDDY I've got it.

EDITH A portent. Forewarning me of the life that lay ahead.

BIDDY And you're not going to believe it. The girl. I knew...

EDITH When you've had a life like mine. When you've lost your own son on an operating table... taken away from you so cruelly and so young... seen the life wrenched from him... before your eyes the vitality snuffed out... And if that weren't agony enough you've had to carry on bringing up another woman's children... children your husband had with the friend you kept too close... Rearing them as your own while your own lies tiny and rotting and cold...

BIDDY Carrick you said her name was? Miss Carrick?

EDITH Nothing you can make up can be worse than reality. These stories were why I became E Nesbit.

BIDDY I know her. Like I said I did. And what a story... What a story I have to tell you about her.

EDITH Of course while I've been living through my darkest days all people have wanted to tell me about is the gift I've given to their healthy happy children. The worlds I've created and joy I've spun. How do you think that makes me feel?

BIDDY Little Miss Carrick. Grown up at last. Well I never. Seems I've got a horror story of my own...

GUASTO No *(in grabbing* **EDITH***'s book)* I have the taste now. Let's have another. Still time before dawn.

EDITH I'm tired. I'm done.

Music. **GUASTO** *picks a story at random.*

GUASTO This one!

EDITH No more...

GUASTO One last chance to keep evil at bay?

BIDDY Edith... I need to tell you something terrible. You have to listen

GUASTO How can you resist?

BIDDY It's important. It could be a matter of life and death.

GUASTO Read!

EDITH *takes the book. Her outburst has left her visibly shaken...*

Scene Four

EDITH A startling story of witchcraft and dark magic... *The Ebony Frame.*

When dear old addled Aunt Dorcas succumbed at long last to the berries of the juniper bush, she left me seven hundred a year and a furnished apartment in a little known Northern spa town.

GUASTO *becomes the narrator.*

GUASTO My initial horror at having to travel so very far soon diminished when I learned the life my new found fortune would allow me to live.

I found her apartment most appealing. It was in the centre of a quaint old town overlooking a stretch of idyllic greenery. I also liked her maid, young Mildred.

EDITH *appears as Mildred.*

Well youngish. But spirited. Perky. Refreshing. I kept on to help around the place.

EDITH Is there anything you'd like adjusting to your quarters sir?

GUASTO I am perfectly happy with the way things are Mildred. But that picture above the mantel. I'm not sure it agrees with my own private tastes.

EDITH *produces an empty ornate black frame.*

EDITH Madam only bought it a while before she died. Mrs Carkshine's Curio Cabinet up on the High Street. Jumped up junk shop so it won't be worth nothing. Said she found it cheery so she did.

GUASTO *reads its title.*

GUASTO Massacre at Tweebosch. A ghastly and graphic depiction of bloody battle.

EDITH She had a leaning towards despair did the mistress. But the frame is in fine fettle. That's the finest ebony.

GUASTO What was in it before this?

EDITH Can't say. Fetched the frame from the attic. There's no end of oddities up there sir. As I say, and I hope you'll forgive me for it, your aunt always had unusual… fascinations.

GUASTO I removed the offending painting and ventured up into the attic where I found another painting abandoned and of the same size as the frame. It was the perfect fit and as I held it I realised it was in fact two paintings sealed together. I prised them apart and to my surprise one was a portrait of me.

GUASTO *holds the frame up to his face and strikes a pose.*

EDITH A very fetching likeness it is too sir. When did you sit for it?

GUASTO I didn't Mildred. Not to my knowledge. My dear aunt must have commissioned it without me being aware. Which is strange. I only saw her once and I'm not even sure she noticed me. She came to London clad in heavy black when I was thirteen and her husband had returned from battling the Boers in a box.

EDITH What's the other painting then?

BIDDY *appears as Elvira, takes the frame and holds it up to her face striking an elegant pose.*

GUASTO I'd never seen eyes like hers before. They commanded as might those of an… Empress.

EDITH Sir. Who is she?

GUASTO I really didn't know. But I hung her image in the ebony frame, which matched the colour of her velvet gown perfectly. My increasing affections for Mildred vanished. I barely noticed her.

EDITH Story of my life.

GUASTO I found I could spend hours alone looking at the mysterious woman from every angle imaginable. I would whisper to her "come down, come down" that's how much I wished she was real.

EDITH But as my old Nan used to say. Be careful what you wish for. For what happened next... well... I still have to pinch myself to make sure it wasn't the worst ever nightmare.

Sinister music...

It were late one night when the master returned unawares he was about to experience something out of this world.

GUASTO I was not drunk, I was not sleepy. I swear what I saw was real. The ebony frame was empty.

EDITH *holds the empty frame.*

And what's more, in a corner of the room shrouded in shadows shifted something darker than night. The fire had burnt low but the thing moved closer. It was her. The woman in the painting.

BIDDY *appears as Elvira.*

BIDDY You called for me. So I am here. And filled with such rapture. I have yearned to see you once more my love. To feel you hold me in your arms.

GUASTO I've never seen you before in my life except in that painting.

BIDDY You told me you'd never love another. I believed you. The way you spoke my name the last night we were together. You were my ruin.

GUASTO I've never ruined anyone.

BIDDY And my salvation.

GUASTO Suddenly I knew… somehow… I knew she was Elvira. Her name was Elvira *(shouting)* Elvira, Elvira, Elvira. How do I know that Elvira?

BIDDY I never thought I'd hear you sat my name again my love.

GUASTO Wait a minute. This is ruddy weird…

BIDDY Why!

GUASTO Why!? I don't know you. But I do. And I did…

BIDDY I can explain.

GUASTO How can there be any explanation…

BIDDY I sold my soul to the devil himself.

GUASTO Oh well there you go…

BIDDY After the night we spent together and you had left I was in turmoil. I had an inkling you wouldn't be true to your word, so I made blood and summoned Mammon the devourer himself. A trick cousin Bethsheba had generously bestowed upon me. After they hung her for it and sliced her in four.

EDITH *is the devil.*

Satan emerged and was conveniently in the guise of a chirpy chamber maid.

EDITH You've been a naughty girl Elvira.

BIDDY And as a sinner I have the right to ask for one wish.

EDITH Are you sure…

GUASTO Be careful what you wish for.

BIDDY I want him to love me for eternity. But he's promised to another. He has to forget her. Leave her. It's me he's meant to be with. Me!

EDITH Let's see. Take this ebony frame. Careful dear. These things were carved at the dawn of time so they aren't ten a penny. As long as your painting stays within it your love will stay true. Now I'll sign for your worthless soul.

Selling of the soul ritual.

BIDDY The devil tricked me!

EDITH Fancy that. And I decided to claim my prize early. I can do that! I'm the devil!

You see my disguise always serve a purpose. My dear Elvira, you're not the first person I've damned dressed like this. The last was a chap who came a cropper through chamber maid me, had decided to keep a rather queer painting of himself up in the attic for decades. Poor fool.

Right. Here goes.

Help, help!! My mistress has gone mad. She's taken to unholy practises.

GUASTO And what happened?

BIDDY I burned as a witch of course. Scorched on the green out yonder then hung drawn and quartered whilst still smouldered.

GUASTO She was bewitching me now. I knew it. But I couldn't resist.

BIDDY Look at the painting of my love. It's you. You must admit. You know it to be true.

GUASTO *appears in the frame.*

The devil is always in the details. And the detail to my deal that the dark master neglected to share was; I would have to wait to mend my broken heart. Wait until the next time you walked this earth. And now at long last fate twisted and sent you to me. Here you are.

GUASTO And now you can be mine.

BIDDY Not as simple as that. You too will have a price to pay.

GUASTO I'm rich beyond my wildest dreams thanks to dead Aunt Dorcas.

BIDDY You're not as bright as you were before. Which is a pity. The price is death. And the loss of your soul.

GUASTO I don't want to die.

BIDDY It will pass in no time. Jump from the window now. There's a carriage coming. If you time it right, as you land it will finish you off. The wheels will cut you in three. The hooves mash out your brains. You won't feel a thing. Jump. Go on jump.

GUASTO No. You must stay here with me. We'll be wed. We'll live out our current lives to their natural end.

BIDDY Impossible.

GUASTO There has to be a way.

BIDDY There isn't. Kill yourself. If you love me die.

GUASTO Please. I don't want to die...

Pause. Elvira hatches a cunning plot.

BIDDY My sweet. There may be a way. It's a risk.

GUASTO Anything...

BIDDY *(angry)* If it were a case of anything our souls would be entwined by now.

Beat.

Forgive me. The eons I've waited and yearned for you. My patience has been tested. Be here at the witching hour tomorrow. Make sure there's no one in the apartment. We need to be alone for my spell to work. If you obey me bliss awaits. We shall finally be together...

She returns to her frame with a wink.

EDITH Meanwhile me, Milly the Maid... the real one... wasn't having this. I'd grown fond of the master. More than fond. I knew something was up and that something weren't right with that ebony frame. Whatever was happening had to do with the wicked looking old cow in the picture.

BIDDY Watch yourself dear.

EDITH See. It's eerie. I could have sworn she talked to me just then.

GUASTO Take a shilling and see a late picture at the Kursaal tonight.

EDITH I went... at least I told him I had.

GUASTO Midnight was nearly upon us. I locked all the doors in the apartment so I couldn't be disturbed. The picture frame was empty. But there was no sign of my Elvira. Then in the same corner of the room where I'd found her again the night before came a shuffle...

EDITH It's me you daft ha'porth. Shinned up the drain pipe and climbed through the window.

GUASTO You can't be here. It won't work...

EDITH What won't? ...Good lord and no mistake. The frame is empty. I knew it. There's witchery afoot.

GUASTO You must leave. I have to be alone. My true love awaits.

EDITH You lummox. She's cursed you into loving her... she's a monster.

Everything in the room shakes. **BIDDY** *appears angry and demonic.*

BIDDY You were meant to be by yourself.

EDITH You still love her now she's looking such a fright?

BIDDY I've warned you missy. Well you're here now, so one more soul for the pot…

> **BIDDY** *snaps out of role and becomes herself.* **EDITH** *and* **GUASTO** *do likewise. This sequence is fast and furious…*

Wait wait…

EDITH Biddy what is it?

BIDDY Miss Carrick. Our mystery girl next door. Her story. It can't wait any longer. It's tragic… terrible…

EDITH You must tell it.

BIDDY I must. For she could well be in terrible danger.

GUASTO *(he's different now. Darker)* Not until we're finished here.

They return to their roles within the tale.

Burning. I smell burning.

BIDDY If you wouldn't kill yourself I've summoned the eternal flame to help you on your way.

The place somehow sets alight… lighting smoke… plastic flames… whatever.

GUASTO I snapped to my senses only to collapse into Mildred's arms.

EDITH I'll get you out of here. Look her painting's alight.

BIDDY *is in the frame contorted in pain.*

BIDDY Stay… you have to stay and be mine…

EDITH I kicked down the doors... if the girls back home who used to chuckle at my chunky ankles could see me now. I dragged the master out and onto the Stray. Looked at his pretty eyes and watched in horror...

That's right. Fill those lungs with good clean air... But he began to writhe in pain as if he were still trapped in the fiery pit that was his home.

GUASTO Mildred. Mildred. My own painting. The image of the man I was when Elvira knew me. You need to save it too.

EDITH But I couldn't go back inside. The place was an inferno.

GUASTO The flames inside devoured the image of my past life hungrily.

I am condemned. Hell bound. Poor me. Have pity. Pity. My soul lost. I am doomed. Doomed.

Light on him as sounds of fire roars around him. He backs away and exits. Lights out.

Scene Five

The lights flicker back up. The tone of our evening has changed. **EDITH** *and* **BIDDY** *are alone and exhausted.* **EDITH** *is anxious sand confused.* **BIDDY** *is close to tears thinking of her own story.*

BIDDY I feel such dread.

EDITH I shouldn't have done this...

BIDDY Such terrible dread, though we're going back... well... eighteen or so long years ago.

EDITH Shouldn't have invited him here.

BIDDY No wonder my memory's been so muddied on the matter.

EDITH In here.

BIDDY And of course when you face something that terrible and blighted...

EDITH I'm lonely. You know Biddy. You're the only one who understands.

BIDDY Your mind has its ways to protect. Preserve your sanity. Help you forget.

EDITH He'll be in with the girl. Quick. Get him.

BIDDY Your tales... oh my... the terror has stirred it all up. The pieces have fallen into place.

EDITH See him off the premises.

BIDDY I need to tell you my story...

EDITH Do it for me.

BIDDY I must tell it...

BIDDY picks up the book. **EDITH** *sees the stark horror in* **BIDDY**'s *eyes. The story starts.*

BIDDY I've been in service for...well... So many families. None as sombre or tragic as the Carrick's. It was long rumoured they were cursed. I was a witness. I knew. These rumours were horribly true.

For years my young master, Grayson Carrick refused to listen to the old legends of his family line. The Carrick's of the present day would only look forward. They'd preserve their energies for future endeavours and happiness. Grayson ignored the warning of his grandmother Agasteena the much feared Carrick matriarch.

EDITH What was her warning?

BIDDY "I have buried my children. Buried my children's children. Because of the Carrick curse. No more... It has to end Grayson. The shadows must be banished. You, who are already destined for an early grave, will be the last of our line."

Agasteena met her maker the day Grayson announced his betrothal to his sweetheart Miss Mabel. Toppled out of her four poster stone dead with a darkness to her tiny eyes before she even reached the floor.

Grayson took me with him and Mabel to their new family home. He was to be away for lengthy spells carrying on the Carrick affairs and Mabel would need a companion. One they could both rely upon. Mabel was a sheer delight. Sweetness itself. But a delicate thing, like a butterfly on a flower. She'd always been sickly and her illnesses had made her femmer but the house Carrick had bought was making her condition worse. Novembertide Hall was gloomy and dark. Not a home for young newlyweds. Not full of life or hope. This was a house of shadows.

When I was alone and walking the corridors I'd get a feeling. Sometimes more than that. I'd sometimes catch a glimpse of something following me from the corner of my eye. The shadows seemed to shift unnaturally, almost as if they were watching and growing and taking on a life of their own.

EDITH But what was the Carrick curse?

BIDDY Several generations before, a Carrick's had killed a young man in a duel. The victim was from a family no one knew much about. Apart from the fact they were noted for their strange ways. They shunned formal religion. There weren't many public places where they found themselves welcome.

The Carrick ancestor died himself a year to the day of his misty dawn duel, only a tortured expression on his face accounting for his demise. Over the following decades the Carrick family were decimated. Fathers, sons, mothers, brothers. No one was safe. All the deaths remained inexplicable. Agasteena Carrick believed the soul of the man who'd been killed was seeking revenge for his own murder. Only when the Carrick line had been snuffed out would his malignant spirit rest.

Whether we believed in spirits walking the earth or not all of us below stairs felt there was something maligned in the walls of Novembertide.

EDITH Did the family stay living at the Hall?

BIDDY Yes. And finally some good news dissipated the shadows. Mabel was with child and the family Doctors felt she was strong enough to bear the child.

EDITH And was she?

BIDDY She gave birth to a beautiful young girl. Lily. My precious Lily. And the shadows lessened. We could breathe more easily as the whole house felt lighter in every way. It wasn't to last.

EDITH What happened?

The shadows creep and take on monstrous forms during the following.

BIDDY One day as mother and child slept in her room the shadows came back darker than ever. They hung in every corner of the house. Crept up every wall... I fled to Mabel's room and opened her door. There at the foot of her bed stood a man of thirty or so, dark haired, immaculately presented, his eyes burning with rage. And as I watched he melted back into shadow. I'd stopped him... I know he hadn't quite carried out what he'd come to do. But he'd still taken a victim.

EDITH Mabel?

BIDDY We put her in the ground. I took up another appointment swiftly. A friend of a friend of the Carrick's. They only had friends of friends. Most steered clear.

EDITH Guasto. Mr Guasto.

BIDDY Never saw the Carrick's again after Mabel's funeral.

EDITH I know where you're lurking.

BIDDY Until Grayson's funeral.

EDITH Guasto...

BIDDY Went the same way. Heart failure they said but I knew by then. I believed in the Carrick Curse and as his second wife sobbed I saw shadows form in the corner of the graveyard. And in their depths I picked out the features of the same handsome man.

EDITH And the baby girl?

BIDDY Haven't you worked it out? The sickly girl lying through there in your spare room now. That's Lily Carrick.

Chimes sound. They both jump.

EDITH Mr Guasto I demand you show yourself at once. Biddy we have to get the intruder out of that room and out of the house...

BIDDY What intruder?

EDITH The young man we've shared the last few hours with?

Pause.

BIDDY You've troubled yourself haven't you?

EDITH Mr Guasto was there. Clear as you are...

BIDDY All the wicked things we've heard tonight.

EDITH He heard them too.

BIDDY I'm blessed not to have your imagination. I can see that now...

EDITH He's been here sitting listening to my stories since we began.

Pause.

BIDDY We've been alone...

EDITH He said, He was here as my admirer.

BIDDY Your private affairs are you own.

EDITH Mr Guasto helped me bring Miss Carrick up from the party.

BIDDY You did that by yourself.

EDITH She fell into his arms...

BIDDY We all saw.

EDITH He lodges with Mrs Fairthought.

BIDDY Lettie Fairthought.

EDITH How am I to know the woman's name?

BIDDY Tuberculosis took her a decade past. Her house was condemned. The whole street was.

EDITH And I kissed him. And he was so very cold. And...

EDITH realises why GUASTO was there. She rushes into the next room. After a few hideous seconds she reappears slowly and in shock.

EDITH He told me my writing had saved his sister....When all the time.

BIDDY No.

EDITH The look in her eyes.

Pause. **BIDDY** *sobs.*

He was here. Don't you realise? I invited him in...

BIDDY And did you see him? Whatever he is. Did you see him Edith? In the dark?

EDITH I very much fear that I did.

Music builds... Behind them GUASTO appears in the doorway. He's backlit and casts a long dark shadow. He and EDITH lock eyes as BIDDY gently sobs.

End

Property List

ACT I

Attic setting (p1 and throughout)
Vase filled with dead lillies (p1)
More vases in the room (p1)
Pile of books (p6)
Velvet cord (p8)
Large book (p10)
Tray with two cups (p12)
Small goblet (p18)
Trunk (p21)
Black confetti (p22)
Eerie looking bridal bouquet (p38)
Plant (p38)

ACT II

The Railway Children book (p42)
Jug (p46)
Gravestone (p49)
Empty ornate black frame (p56)

Lighting

ACT I

The lights flicker (p9)
Lights flicker again (p11)
Biddy turns out the gas lights (p14)
Lightning hones in on Edith (p14)
Darker (p22)
Lights flicker back up (p24)

Unnerving light effect (p35)
Stage goes black (p36)
Lights up on Guasto as Amelia(p36)
Lights up on Edith (p39)
Light change (p39)
Lights out (p41)

ACT II

Light only on Edith as she reads (p42)
Light comes up (p43)
Place sets alight with lighting smoke, plastic flames (p63)
Light on Guasto (p64)
Lights out (p64)
Lights flicker back up (p65)
Lighting effect of creeping shadows (p68)
Shadows creep and take on monstrous forms (p71)
Guasto backlit and casting a long dark shadow (p74)

Sound Effects

ACT I

If performing at Christmas play God Rest Ye Merry Gentlemen (p1)
Festive gathering, bursts of music and muffled laughter (p1)
Chimes from somewhere (p4)
Wind howls outside (p11)
Very loud bang as Biddy enters the room (p12)
Midnight strikes (p14)
Carols of the Bells begin to play (p14)
Music (p18)
Music stops (p19)
Sound of a bike bell (p19)

Music for passage of time (p20)
Sound of a bike bell (p20)
Church bells peel (p21)
Unsettling organ music (p22)
Bike ring (p22)
Music reaches a crescendo (p24)
Music (p28)
Big slam (p36)
Deep terrifying screams (p36)
Guggling chuckles from a vampire plant (p36)
An eerie sound – like the name Amelia being called (p37)
Eerie voice sounds Amelia, Amelia (p37)
Hear the voice again (p38)
A chime (p40)
Music starts (p41)
Music (p41)

ACT II

Vivid sound effects (p42)

Sound of crashing an explosion and the children screaming (p43)

Chimes (p43)

Music – Christmas music played on a creepy street organ (p48)

Sound of young girls laughing (p48)

Music of the street organ but fainter (p50)

Music (p53)

The music builds (p53)

Sinister music (p58)

Sound of fire roars around him (p64)

Silent Night playing in the distance (p71)

Chimes (p72)

Music builds (p74)

www.ingramcontent.com/pod-product-compliance
Ingram Content Group UK Ltd.
Pitfield, Milton Keynes, MK11 3LW, UK
UKHW021840210426
5322IPUK00022B/392